# Unraveling the Dark Web

## *An Insightful Exploration*

# Table of Contents

# Chapter 1. Introduction

In this illuminating Special Report, we invite you to join us on a journey deep into the mysteries of the digital universe. "Unraveling the Dark Web: An Insightful Exploration", is a comprehensive yet accessible examination of one of the most enigmatic aspects of our digital age. While the subject might seem foreboding or excessively technical, fear not. Our experts delicately dissect this complex web, rendering it understandable for every reader. We decipher the concealed labyrinth of the Dark Web, shedding light on its origins, operations, and intriguing uses. Whether you're a tech enthusiast curious to extend your frontier of knowledge, a newbie determined to bolster your understanding, or a concerned parent or individual aiming to stay safe online, this report is exactly what you've been waiting for. Open the pages, and dive straight into the mysterious underbelly of the internet; who knows what fascinating realities you may uncover! Trust us, this is one journey you would not want to miss.

# Chapter 2. The Genesis and Evolution of the Dark Web

In an ever-evolving ecosystem of technological advancements, a moniker that often raises eyebrows is the "Dark Web". This nebulous portion of the internet is layered in mystery, misunderstood by many, and yet forms a crucial part of understanding our digital world.

## 2.1. The Birth of The Dark Web

The roots of the Dark Web can be traced back to the late 1960s. The Department of Defense's Advanced Research Projects Agency (DARPA) developed ARPANET (Advanced Research Projects Agency Network), arguably the ancestor of the modern internet. It was a private network connecting universities and governmental establishments, designed to withstand a nuclear attack. A decentralized network model ensured that communication could proceed unhindered even if parts of the network were destroyed.

In the early 1970s, ARPANET adopted TCP/IP (Transmission Control Protocol/Internet Protocol), making network interactions more standardized and efficient. This played a fundamental role in enabling the birth of the internet as we know it today.

However, it wasn't until the 1990s that what we now call the 'Dark Web' began to take shape. Researchers from the U.S Army and Navy developed the concept for Tor network (originally standing for The Onion Router) as a means to protect governmental surfaces' communications. This was further developed by DARPA in the 1990s into larger scale, being utilized by the broader public from 2004.

## 2.2. Emergence of Anonymity

Tor pioneered the use of 'onion routing' – a method that enabled anonymous communication over a computer network. It involved encapsulating data in several layers of encryption (hence the 'onion' metaphor), encrypted and decrypted in multiple stages, ensuring anonymity. Users could access the internet without exposing their location or other potentially identifiable information.

Over the years, more tools and services emerged that afforded anonymity to its users, with Invisible Internet Project (I2P), FreeNet, ZeroNet, and others joining the fold, further expanding the Dark Web.

## 2.3. Rise of the Darknet Marketplaces

In 2011, the Dark Web took a notorious turn with the launch of Silk Road, the first and most infamous darknet marketplace. It allowed users to buy and sell illegal items, primarily drugs, using Bitcoin for transactions to maintain pervading anonymity.

Silk Road was shut down by law enforcement in 2013, but it sparked a rise of other darknet marketplaces such as AlphaBay, Agora, and Dream Market. Despite constant crackdown by law enforcement agencies, new darknet markets regularly emerge, being an ongoing cat and mouse game.

## 2.4. Beyond the Illicit

Despite its infamy, the Dark Web is not merely a hive of illicit activity. The technology behind it had a deeper purpose: privacy. Many individuals and organizations worldwide use the Dark Web for entirely benign or even positive activities. Journalists utilize it to communicate with whistleblowers, activists skirt surveillance in oppressive regimes, and some people simply prefer the added layer of privacy.

## 2.5. Shaping the Future

The Dark Web continues to evolve, responding to advancements in technology and shifts in societal attitudes towards privacy and freedom of information. Tor, for example, has grown well beyond its initial military use-case, providing access to millions of users every day who prefer privacy over surveillance.

The emergence of newer technologies like blockchain and cryptocurrencies, which inherently offer greater anonymity, leaves the Dark Web poised to adapt and expand further. Their potential integration with Dark Web technologies could redefine internet privacy, cybersecurity, and digital rights as we know them.

Yet, alongside its positive uses, its potential to serve malicious aims can't be understated. The Dark Web will continue to be the focus of ongoing tension between privacy advocates, lawmakers, and those using its capabilities for nefarious deeds.

While this journey through the genesis and evolution of the Dark Web only scratches the surface, it serves to provide an understanding of its origins, evolution, and impact on the digital world. Its future remains uncharted territory, continually shaped by technological advancements, societal norms, and regulatory pressures. As we delve further into the 21st century, the Dark Web's trajectory will continue to provide a fascinating case study of technological innovation versus societal need for protection.

# Chapter 3. Unmasking the Veil: Understanding the Dark Web Infrastructure

At the heart of the digital universe, there lies a well-kept secret: the Dark Web. Commonly misunderstood and often associated with illegal activities, it remains something of an enigma to the everyday internet user. The Dark Web, in fact, forms an integral part of the broader web infrastructure - a part we wouldn't encounter during our typical online routines. Its foundational elements - onions, TOR, privacy, encryption, and freedom - combine, leading us to an intriguing, yet often intimidating, world in the depths of the cyber cosmos.

## 3.1. What is the Dark Web?

In a nutshell, the Dark Web (also known as the 'Darknet') forms a tiny yet crucial portion of the deep web. To understand this, imagine an iceberg. The part visible to any observer symbolizes the Surface Web - the part of the internet accessible via popular search engines such as Google. However, almost 90% of the iceberg lays concealed below the water surface, which stands for the Deep Web: a vast expanse of information and data which cannot be indexed by traditional search engines. And within the deep, shadowy abyss of the Deep Web, exists a fraction known as the Dark Web.

Importantly, Dark Web isn't inherently evil or illicit. It's merely a section of the web largely inaccessible via conventional means. This feature contributes to its appeal in various sectors: for activists living under oppressive governments, whistle-blowers, or researchers seeking to bypass censorship restrictions, to name a few.

# 3.2. The Onion Routing (TOR)

The primary tool essential for navigating through the Dark Web is The Onion Router, or TOR. Adeptly named, TOR uses the Onion Routing technique where data encryption is done in multiple layers, similar to the layers of an onion.

When a TOR user sends a request, the data is first encrypted on their system and then sent through a series of relays, each of which removes a single layer of encryption. This multilayered mechanism ensures the identity of the users and the content remains anonymous and secure.

# 3.3. The Intricacies of The TOR Network

The TOR network comprises volunteer-operated servers distributed around the world. When you send a request via TOR, the information does not travel directly from the sender to the receiver. Instead, it gets bounced around the numerous servers, or NODES, in the TOR network.

Each hop in this journey is randomized, which means even if someone were tracking an individual piece of data, they would find it an incredibly complex task to trace back to the originating IP address. As the information passes through each node, one layer of encryption is shed, and by the end of the journey, the request stands in its original form.

# 3.4. Hidden Services

The Dark Web is home to numerous hidden services marked by their .onion domain. These .onion sites exist solely within the TOR network and cannot be accessed via typical browsers or search engines.

Among the most well-known of these hidden services is 'The Hidden Wiki,' an information portal providing links to other onion sites across the Dark Web.

Such diversified use symbolizes the dual-edged nature of the Dark Web – it facilitates certain measures of freedom and security, but can also serve as a breeding ground for illegal activities.

## 3.5. Dark Web and Cryptocurrency

Cryptocurrency, particularly Bitcoin, is the leading mode of transaction on the Dark Web. Its widespread adoption is largely due to the anonymity and ease of transactions it affords its users, making it an inevitable part of the Dark Web infrastructure.

However, it's worth noting that blockchain, the underlying technology of Bitcoin, leaves behind a transaction trail, which, if pursued with tenacity, could potentially lead curious minds to the transaction participants.

## 3.6. Staying Safe

The Dark Web, as alluring as it may be to the curious mind, can also be a perilous place. Malwares, scams, questionable content and services abound, and users could potentially be exposed to legal risks. Hence, a practical approach to safety is paramount. Avoid revealing personal information, be cautious of downloading files or clicking dubious links, and stay within legal boundaries.

In conclusion, while the Dark Web seems to emanate an aura of the forbidden and unknown, it is, fundamentally, another tool on the Internet – a tool whose use can lead to paths of liberation or incarceration, depending on how one uses it. So venture with care, and remember that every tool is only as benevolent, or malevolent, as the hands that wield it.

# Chapter 4. The Good, the Bad, and the Ugly: Uses of the Dark Web

The digital world is often likened to an iceberg. The visible internet, which most of us access daily, constitutes just the tip of the iceberg. Below the surface, however, lies the vast, unindexed territory which is the Deep and Dark Web. Its uses are myriad, encompassing both the good and the bad. Let's dive in and try to untangle this complex web of digital phenomenons.

## 4.1. The Good: Beacon of Free Speech and Privacy

The Dark Web's anonymizing features provide a haven for free speech, privacy, and even safety. It fosters a space where political dissidents, whistleblowers, and journalists can communicate without fear of retaliation or censorship. Here, conscientious objectors can make their voices heard.

One prime example of this is the whistleblower Edward Snowden who famously leaked classified information from the National Security Agency (NSA). His disclosures ignited global discussions about privacy, surveillance, and the reach of state intelligence. The Dark Web has proven to be pivotal in such cases, facilitating secure and anonymous information sharing routes.

Another admirable use of the Dark Web is protecting persecuted groups. In oppressive regimes where internet use is either heavily censored or monitored, the Dark Web often provides the only viable platform for political dissent and organizing opposition.

In addition, researchers and investigators often use the Dark Web for gathering intelligence and counter-terrorism studies. Its disquieting encrypted spaces host valuable insights that could potentially save lives.

## 4.2. The Bad: Illicit Trade and Cybercrime

Unsurprisingly, the Dark Web has gained notoriety for illegal activities. Its anonymity makes it perfect for illicit trades. It has birthed infamous platforms like Silk Road, AlphaBay, and Hansa, where transactions encompassed drugs, firearms, counterfeit currencies, stolen data, and even hiring assassins.

Silk Road, for instance, was the first Darknet Market (DNM) that operated as a Tor hidden service. Before it was shut down, it had amassed over a million users, and its legacy is still felt today in the persistent presence of various DNMs.

Stolen personal data is another huge market. Credit card information, social security numbers, and other sensitive data are sold for nefarious purposes. Cyberattacks, too, often begin here, with hacking tools and ransomware readily available for purchase.

## 4.3. The Ugly: Exploitation and Human Misery

Beyond illegal trade, darker corners of the Dark Web host deeply disturbing content—human trafficking, child exploitation, and grotesque acts of violence. Again, the anonymity offered fuels these horrifying aspects, making it difficult for authorities to track down the culprits.

There are cases though, where law enforcement agencies have

managed to unmask such activities, as with the notorious Playpen case where the FBI tracked down and arrested the operators of a horrific child exploitation site. Nevertheless, the fight against such atrocities is far from straightforward due to the technological challenges and international jurisdictions involved.

The Dark Web is a product of the internet era — unchecked and rampant, befitting its appellation 'Wild West of the Internet.' However, it continually demands our attention and understanding. By knowing what lurks beneath the surface, agencies, organizations, and individual users can tread more wisely in the digital world, learning to harness the good, combat the bad, and condemn the ugly.

# Chapter 5. Of Bits and Bytes: Technical Protocols of the Dark Web

To commence our understanding of the Dark Web, it's vital to tackle the underlying technical protocols which form the digital backbone of this encrypted realm. This first section, therefore, portays an in-depth examination of these technical protocols anchoring the operations of the Dark Web.

The inception of the Internet, originally designed for free and seamless communication, saw various protocols emerge - the foundational codes governing Internet communications. Aptly named "Internet Protocol," or IP, it became the primary method for sending and receiving messages online. Imagine an IP address as your home address on the vast global Internet.

However, with privacy and security concerns surfacing, our digital community fell upon a need for anonymized communication, whence sprang forth the concept of the Dark Web.

## 5.1. The Tor Network and Onion Routing

Foremost among the Dark Web infrastructure is "The Onion Router," or Tor, so named for its layers of encryption, similar to the layers in an onion. A creation of the U.S. Navy, and now an open-source project, Tor is the most prevalent protocol employed for accessing the Dark Web.

Tor ensures data privacy by implementing the practice of 'Onion Routing'. As data travels through the Tor network, it's not a straightforward point A to point B journey. Instead, the data is encrypted and then passed through multiple volunteer-operated servers — or 'nodes'. Each node peels back one layer of encryption to discover the data's next destination. This loop of encryption and decryption continues till the data reaches the final node, called the 'exit node'.

The identities of the data sender and the final receiver remain concealed; nodes only know their immediate previous and next connection in the chain, but never the complete journey. Thus, an individual's online footprint gets buried under layers of encryption, making their activity on the Dark Web inherently anonymous.

With Tor, 'www' web addresses shift to '.onion' URLs, only accessible through the Tor browser. This accessibility constraint further strengthens the obscurity of the Dark Web.

# 5.2. The Invisible Internet Project (I2P)

I2P, or the Invisible Internet Project, is another communication protocol used in the Dark Web. Similar to Tor, I2P provides a layer of protection and anonymity to its users. However, unlike Tor, which uses exit nodes to interact with the regular Internet, the I2P network caters exclusively to internal anonymous or "hidden" services.

I2P employs 'garlic routing,' a variant of 'onion routing.' It bundles multiple messages together, which adds an additional level of complexity, making it more secure but a bit slower.

# 5.3. Virtual Private Networks (VPN)

Although not exclusively a Dark Web protocol, VPNs add an additional layer of security when coupled with Tor or I2P. A VPN masks your IP address, making it appear as if your Internet activity originates from a different location. This additional step fortifies your anonymity, especially when accessing the Dark Web.

## 5.4. Cryptographic Practices

Cryptography plays an instrumental role in the technical protocols of the Dark Web. Cryptography, in essence, is a method of protecting information by transforming it into an unreadable format. Only those with special knowledge, usually termed as a 'key', can read it.

In the context of the Dark Web, the Secure Socket Layer (SSL) or Transport Layer Security (TLS) protocols are crucial for securing communications. They establish an encrypted link between a web server and a browser, ensuring all data passed between them remain private.

## 5.5. Special Browsers: Tor, I2P and Freenet

Special browsers are needed to access the Dark Web, with different browsers catering to different networks. The Tor browser is most popularly used, but for the I2P network, their own I2P browser is necessitated. Freenet, another 'darknet', also requires a specially dedicated Freenet browser.

Moreover, configurations and precautions are required when using these browsers to maintain the highest degree of anonymity, that includes changing certain habits of traditional web browsing as well.

## 5.6. Future Technical Developments

As privacy concerns and the demand for anonymity grow, new protocols and techniques continue to emerge. This includes next-gen anonymity networks offering stronger security and more robust infrastructure. The exploration of quantum-safe algorithms also open a new frontier to protect against future threats from quantum computing.

In conclusion, the Dark Web is a complex matrix of protocols, networks, and encryption techniques. However, it's this complexity that enables it to provide a secure and anonymous platform for its users. It's these building blocks of bits and bytes that make the Dark Web what it is: a mysterious, encrypted world seemingly lurking in the shadows of the digital universe.

# Chapter 6. Color of Shadows: Distinguishing between the Surface Web, Deep Web, and Dark Web

Before venturing further into the enigma of the Dark Web, let's establish a comprehensive understanding of the three main layers of the internet. These are the Surface Web, the Deep Web, and the Dark Web.

## 6.1. The Surface Web

Chances are, the part of the internet you interact with daily is termed as the Surface Web, also known as the Clearweb or Visible Web. This layer embodies all the information that is indexed and can be tracked or searched using traditional search engines like Google, Bing, Yahoo, etc.

The Surface Web follows HTTPS/HTTP protocols and is accessible through regular browsers. Sites such as news portals, e-Commerce platforms, blogs, social media, etc., all fall under this category. However, despite being the most frequented part of our online experience, it constitutes just about 4% of the total internet –a mere tip of the digital iceberg.

## 6.2. The Deep Web

Beneath the Surface Web, stretching to virtual depths far greater than imaginable, lies the Deep Web. What sets the Deep Web apart is its unindexed nature. This vast online space comprises academic databases, governmental records, medical archives, organizations' private databases, etc., that 'traditional' search engines can't access.

The Deep Web works on HTTPS/HTTP protocols and is, theoretically, accessible through ordinary web browsers. However, its contents remain password-protected or encrypted. This is where your online banking details, personal email data, and subscription specifics reside. Importantly, it houses approximately 96% of the data on the internet, making the Surface Web a very small portion by comparison.

# 6.3. The Dark Web

Further into the abyss lies the Dark Web –a fraction of the Deep Web shrouded in layers of encryption and anonymity. It's here where the internet sheds its skin of oversight and traceability. This portion of the Web operates on a network overlay of servers, in which connections are established between trusted peers only, using non-standard protocols and ports.

Tor (The Onion Router) is the most commonly used software to access this part of the internet, ensuring anonymity by bouncing encrypted data around numerous servers globally before it reaches its final destination. Other software like I2P and Freenet also provide similar services. While it's synonymous with nefarious activities due to its impenetrable nature, it is important to remember that it is also used for legitimate purposes like circumventing censorship, activism, secure communications and ensuring privacy free from surveillance.

These shadows of the internet might seem different shades of grey, but they are inherently distinguished by their levels of accessibility, purpose and commonly, misconception.

# 6.4. Surface Web: Here and Clear

Contrary to popular notion, the Surface Web is not merely a

playground for cat videos, online shopping, or scrolling through for dinner recipes. It serves a range of significant purposes such as disseminating information, functioning as a platform for online learning, acting as an avenue for commercial transactions, and providing social networking platforms, among others.

The primary characteristic of the Surface Web is its indexability into search engine databases. This accessibility and visibility are why it is often associated with an 'iceberg's tip'. It is critical to remember that while the Surface Web is easily perceptible, it constitutes a surprisingly small part of the actual internet.

## 6.5. Diving into the Deep Web

Moving deeper into the Ocean of Data, the Deep Web is aptly named, housing endless scrolls of unindexed and often sensitive data. These include password-protected content such as online banking information, membership websites, paid content on media portals, email servers, and a multitude of databases.

The pervasive misconception surrounds the Deep Web as a hub for illicit activities; in truth, it serves several respectable purposes. Any tightknit data storage protected from indexing falls into this category. It is the safeguarding of personal data, a concept of increasing importance in our digital world. It is also a repository for historical information, research data, sensitive governmental documents, and more. In essence, it is the invisible majority of the internet.

## 6.6. The Enigma of the Dark Web

The Dark Web, the most elusive part of our digital realm, often sensationalized, is a popular topic feeding our collective imagination. A small portion of the Deep Web, the Dark Web thrives on anonymity and obscurity. Information is neither indexed nor easily accessible gives it a somewhat notorious reputation.

Yes, there is an element of truth to its infamous reputation. The Dark Web hosts a significant percentage of illicit activities, including black markets, forums for hackers, and the grimier corners of humanity. However, it should not diminish the fact that the Dark Web is also a secure communication channel for journalists, dissidents, and whistle-blowers who live under repressive regimes or fear reprisals.

## 6.7. In Conclusion

The Surface Web, Deep Web, and Dark Web each have utility and purpose, painting them in black and white or characterizing them merely as 'good' or 'bad' would be an oversimplification. The internet, like every tool mankind has ever constructed, mirrors the myriad facets of its creators, us. It can be a space for information or miscommunication, liberation or subjugation, crime or justice –a function of one's intent and purpose.

As you journey around this expansive universe, equipped with a deeper understanding, it becomes apparent - it's not the darkness of the Web that we grapple with, but the shadows within ourselves reflected there.

# Chapter 7. Dark Marketplaces and Cryptocurrencies: The Economy of the Dark Web

The Dark Web is renowned as a hub for unfettered and unregulated economic activity. The most infamous manifestation of this comes in the form of Dark Marketplaces. These platforms serve as conduits for all kinds of goods and services, legal and illicit alike.

## 7.1. Understanding Dark Marketplaces

Dark marketplaces are essentially the black markets of the digital realm. They function similarly to conventional online marketplaces, with suppliers, customers, and facilitators. However, the similarities largely end there; instead of books or furniture, these platforms traffic in things like illegal drugs, stolen data, and counterfeit money.

These platforms thrive due to three key elements: anonymity, an untraceable form of payment, and a willing community. The most significant element, perhaps, is anonymity. Leveraging onion routing techniques, a type of online navigation that obscures user identities and actions, suppliers and consumers engage in transactions without revealing any identifiable details.

The untraceable form of payment is typically undertaken through cryptocurrencies, most notably Bitcoin. Additionally, these marketplaces house a thriving community of individuals willing to both supply and purchase illicit goods and services. Regulating such businesses can be quite challenging, as new ones rapidly replace those that law enforcement agencies manage to shut down.

# 7.2. Cryptocurrencies: Fueling the Dark Economy

Cryptocurrencies, decentralized forms of digital or virtual currency, have become the de facto currency of the Dark Web, particularly the dark marketplaces. Their decentralized nature and the anonymity they provide make them ideal for such transactions. Bitcoin, the first and the most well-known cryptocurrency, has been extensively used in these marketplaces, overshadowing traditional forms of payment such as credit cards and wire transfers.

However, over the years, as Bitcoin transactions became more traceable, other cryptocurrencies such as Monero and Zcash have gained popularity due to their enhanced privacy features.

Let's explore some major reasons why cryptocurrencies dominate the economic landscape of the Dark Web:

1. **Anonymity**: The primary attraction of cryptocurrencies is the layer of anonymity they provide to users. While Bitcoin transactions can now be traced back to users, other options offer totally private transactions.

2. **Global Usage**: Cryptocurrencies can be used globally without any exchange rates, fees, or governmental red tape, which aids the seamless trade of goods and services across international borders.

3. **Decentralization**: The decentralized nature of cryptocurrencies means that they aren't controlled by any government or institution. This makes them immune to governmental policies and sanctions, a significant advantage for those operating in the grey sectors of the economy.

While these features make cryptocurrencies an ideal financial tool for dark marketplaces, they also pose significant risks. Cryptocurrencies are notoriously volatile, subject to sudden drastic fluctuations in value, and are prone to theft by hackers. Moreover, despite their perceived anonymity, law enforcement agencies are developing technologies and strategies to track transactions conducted using these digital assets.

## 7.3. Rise and Fall of Famous Dark Marketplaces

Several dark marketplaces have risen and fallen over time. The pioneer was an underground website called "Silk Road," established in 2011. This platform managed to build a considerable customer base by providing an easy-to-use interface and a wide variety of illicit goods. However, the rampant illegal activities conducted on the Silk Road drew the attention of law enforcement agencies, leading to its eventual shutdown in 2013.

However, the void left by Silk Road triggered an explosion in the number of dark marketplaces. Some of them, like AlphaBay and Dream Market, had several thousand listings spanning various illegal goods and services. These larger markets have since been closed, often due to law enforcement efforts, but many smaller markets remain active and continue to facilitate illicit trade.

## 7.4. The Challenge of Regulation and the Future

Regulating dark marketplaces is a significant challenge. Even if one marketplace is shut down, several others take its place. Anonymity and the use of untraceable currencies make finding and prosecuting perpetrators challenging.

The future of these dark marketplaces is uncertain. On one hand, improved privacy features of newer cryptocurrencies like Monero could aid the growth of these platforms. On the other hand, increased scrutiny and improved methods of tracking illegal activities by law enforcement agencies could limit their expansion.

In the end, the dark marketplaces serve as a stark reminder of the drastic effects technology can have on our society. It is a demonstration of how technologies that can be beneficial, like cryptocurrencies and secure browsing, can also be exploited to no good end.

This concludes our exploration of the dark marketplaces and cryptocurrencies. It's clear that as long as the desire for illicit goods and services exists, and as long as technology provides an avenue for that desire to be met, there's little doubt that these shadowy digital bazaars will continue to exist in one form or another. It's a game of cat and mouse, with law enforcement and black market operators continually evolving to one-up each other. As an observer, all we can do is wait and see how this fascinating struggle plays out.

# Chapter 8. Anonymity and Freedom: The Appeal of the Dark Web

When it comes to the Dark Web, anonymity and freedom are among its prime offerings, but they are also its loudest critiques. Darkness, as ominous as it sounds, provides a veil of anonymity that users find both appealing and necessary. After all, privatization around the World Wide Web is quickly dwindling, leading some to seek refuge in the clouded depths of the Dark Web.

## 8.1. The Magnet of Anonymity

The Dark Web's anonymity is mainly facilitated through the use of TOR, The Onion Router. Just as layers of an onion conceal its core, TOR networks shield a user's identity by wrapping their Internet Protocol (IP) addresses in numerous layers of encrypted, rerouted data. These layers make it extremely challenging for third parties to trace the source or destination of the information. The transformed IP addresses generally appear random and indistinguishable from ordinary web traffic.

This protection provides a safe haven for numerous parties, ranging from privacy-conscious individuals and whistleblowers, to journalists working in restrictive regimes, and unfortunately, to cybercriminals. The TOR network offers a level of assurance that their real identities remain concealed, allowing them to express their opinions, share sensitive information, or conduct their activities without the fear of retribution.

# 8.2. Freedom: A Double-Edged Sword

Freedom is perhaps the Dark Web's most controversial aspect. On one hand, it abounds in possibilities and liberation by enabling users to bypass censorship. Various press freedom organizations advocate for the use of TOR and other similar technologies for journalists and activists working under oppressive governments, where surveillance and censorship are commonplace. A glimpse into this life-saving potential reveals that the Dark Web can act as a champion of free speech and independence.

However, the same freedom also gives free rein to harmful activities. Illegal drug trading, Arms dealing, human trafficking, identity theft, and child exploitation thrive on the Dark Web, hidden beneath the layers of anonymity. Transgressions like these lead critics to demand regulation of this murky corner of the Internet, despite the logistical and ethical complexities such a task would entail.

# 8.3. A Mechanism for Whistleblowing

One of the unquestionably positive uses of the Dark Web's anonymity is its role in facilitating whistleblowing. Websites like SecureDrop, a submission system facilitated by the Freedom of the Press Foundation, allow whistleblowers to upload classified or sensitive documents anonymously.

In such scenarios, the Dark Web serves as a catalyst for societal change, exposing corruption and holding power accountable. For instance, Edward Snowden, a famous whistleblower, utilized TOR networks to leak classified information from the National Security Agency (NSA), throwing light on heavy-handed state surveillance techniques and sparking fierce debates on privacy rights across the globe.

# 8.4. The Cost of Anonymity

Nevertheless, anonymity and freedom come at a cost. Performance is a key compromise users make when utilizing TOR networks. Encrypted connections considerably slow down browsing speed, resulting in a less-than-optimal user experience.

In addition to the use of darknet markets for illicit activities, the anonymity offered by the Dark Web also permits the proliferation of revenge porn, Doxing (publicly revealing previously anonymous personal information), Swatting (deceiving emergency services into sending an emergency response to another person's address), and other cyber-harassment acts.

These threats, along with the risk of stumbling onto disturbing content, make Dark Web exploration perilous for the unprepared user.

# 8.5. Anonymity vs Privacy: A Need for Distinction

An important nuance to be aware of is the distinction between anonymity and privacy. Privacy generally involves withholding personal information from being accessed or disclosed. Anonymity, on the other hand, involves disguising one's identity.

Both aspects are essential in securing the rights of individuals on the Internet. The Dark Web allows both of these aspects to flourish, creating a space where people can associate, express, and interact without fear of repercussion or persecution.

# 8.6. In Conclusion

In the end, the discussion of anonymity and freedom in the Dark Web is a conversation fraught with moral, ethical, and practical complexities. It is a critical part of the larger ongoing discourse on the intricacies of internet governance, the right to privacy and free speech, and the ethical limits of state and corporate surveillance.

While the Dark Web is undoubtedly a hub for some of the most abhorrent and despicable activities, it is also a vital tool for dissidents, activists, and those living under oppressive regimes. Striking the right balance between regulation and freedom, while maintaining the notion of individual privacy, is one of the greatest challenges the digital world faces today. In that sense, understanding the intricacy and the nuance of the Dark Web is integral for anyone aiming to comprehend the modern digital landscape.

# Chapter 9. Cybersecurity Issues and the Dark Web: A Complex Coexistence

To fully appreciate the complexities of the Dark Web and its connection with cybersecurity issues, it is essential to understand its organic relationship with the Internet. This interconnected digital universe where we consume and produce immense volumes of data has intrinsic vulnerabilities, some of which are exploited by Dark Web activities. In this chapter, we delve into these vulnerabilities, how the Dark Web capitalizes on them, and the cybersecurity measures necessary to ensure your digital safety.

## 9.1. Understanding Dark Web Vulnerabilities

Primarily, it's key to establish a rudimentary understanding of what the Dark Web is and how it operates. The Dark Web, also known as the 'hidden internet,' is an overlay network within the Internet that is accessed only with specific software, configurations, or authorization. It forms a small but significant part of the Deep Web, a broader subset of the Internet not indexed by search engines.

The Dark Web is often associated with illegal activities, yet it also serves permissible purposes, like supporting free speech and facilitating confidential communication channels for whistleblowers. However, it must be acknowledged that its anonymous nature and unregulated framework make it a perfect breeding ground for potentially malicious endeavors.

A significant portion of cybercriminals exploits these favorable conditions, making cyber threats an inevitable part of the Dark Web's existence. These cyber threats can range from relatively minor cybercrimes like phishing and malware attacks, right through to the higher end of the cybercrime spectrum which includes data breaches, denial of service attacks, and advanced persistent threats.

## 9.2. The Many Faces of Dark Web Cyber Threats

1. **Phishing**:

Phishing is a simple yet highly effective tactic, involving cybercriminals posing as legitimate entities to deceive their victims into revealing sensitive information, such as usernames, passwords, and credit card numbers.

1. **Malware**:

Malware, or malicious software, is designed to cause damage or unauthorized access to a computer, network, or the entire infrastructure. It encompasses a variety of forms, including viruses, worms, Trojans, ransomware, and spyware. The Dark Web often acts as a repository where cybercriminals distribute malware.

1. **Data breaches**:

Data breaches on the Dark Web involve unauthorized access, copying, transmission, or use of sensitive information. Information often targeted includes personal identification, financial records, health records, or proprietary business data. Stolen data can be traced back to the Dark Web where it may be sold or traded.

1. **Denial of Service (DoS) attacks and Distributed Denial of Service (DDoS) attacks**:

These attacks aim to make resources, such as a network, server or website, unavailable to intended users. Cybercriminals often leverage the Dark Web to organize these attacks, coordinate botnets, or trade exploitation tools and techniques.

1. **Advanced Persistent Threats (APTs)**:

APTs are long-term, calculated attacks where cybercriminals gain and maintain unauthorized access to a network to mine highly sensitive information. They often occur in the realms of nation-states and large corporations, implying high-level sophistication and resources.

# 9.3. Counteracting Cyber Threats

How, then, can we counteract these threats? Achieving cybersecurity isn't about waging a one-off battle but an ongoing war involving continually evolving security practices.

1. **Prevention is the Best Cure**:

The initial step in bolstering cybersecurity is awareness and prevention. This includes creating strong, unique passwords, employing multi-factor authentication, keeping software up-to-date, and learning to identify and avoid potential phishing attacks.

1. **Regular Data Back-ups:**

Backing up data is no longer a recommended option, but a critical part of a robust cybersecurity strategy. Regular data assessments and backups can mitigate data loss in incidents such as ransomware attacks.

1. **Implement Security Software:**

Quality security software serves as a trusted front line defense against threats, providing active protection against hostile activities, automatic defense updates, and real-time threat detection.

1. **Education:**

Once the basics are in place, continuous education is essential. We should strive to remain up-to-date regarding emerging threats and common vulnerabilities.

1. **Professional Help:**

Sometimes, knowledge alone is insufficient. Depending on the nature of the information at stake, it might be beneficial to hire experts to analyze, enhance, and maintain your cybersecurity defenses.

# 9.4. Looking to the Future

Ensuring cybersecurity isn't just about implementing robust protocols; it's about fostering a culture of security. With the Dark Web's coexistence with everyday internet interaction, understanding its characteristics and actuating thorough defense mechanisms remain key to the digital universe's healthy evolution.

The evolution of technology is perpetual, and with it, so are the accompanying threats. While the Dark Web continues to harbor these vulnerabilities, it also forces us to evolve, reassess our defenses, and stay continually informed. Ultimately, navigating this realm goes beyond battling cyber threats. It is about safeguarding the digital universe's integrity, acting responsibly, and adopting proactive measures to ensure our shared digital futures are as secure as possible.

# Chapter 10. Lessons from the Dark Web: How to Improve Privacy and Security Online

The Dark Web, often painted in shades of disconcerting grey, can paradoxically offer vital lessons on improving our online privacy and security. Beside its notorious reputation, the tools and techniques that prop up this hidden segment of the internet play a significant role in maintaining user anonymity.

## 10.1. Understanding the Importance of Anonymity

Firstly, recognizing the criticalness of online anonymity is essential. In the world of the Dark Web, anonymity is not simply a preference. It's a fundamental requirement. The methods employed by Dark Web users to achieve this level of obscurity can be applied to our daily internet usage for enhanced privacy.

Let's observe VPNs (Virtual Private Networks) - a commonly used technology in the Dark Web. VPNs encrypt your data and mask your online activities by directing your Internet traffic through a specially configured remote server. This process, known as "tunneling", prevents your Internet Service Provider (ISP), hackers, or government entities from surveilling your online habits. Outside the Dark Web, deploying a VPN can make you far less susceptible to cyber threats and reduces the potential of personal data leakage.

# 10.2. Profiting from End-to-End Encryption

Another concept routinely employed in the Dark Web is end-to-end encryption, where only the communicating users can read the messages. The Dark Web thrives on such, especially within various messaging platforms. Implementing similar forms of encryption in personal or professional messaging can significantly upsurge our security, preventing unauthorized intrusion.

End-to-end encryption is like sending a sealed letter: only the recipient can open it and read the contents. Common messaging apps like WhatsApp and Signal leverage this type of encryption. It means that no third party can decrypt and read your messages, not even the company that owns the platform.

# 10.3. Leveraging Tor for Anonymity

Next, we turn to The Onion Router (Tor), another vital tool associated with the Dark Web. Tor is as an open-source software program that allows users to browse the web anonymously. It does this by routing your internet connection through several servers across the globe, making it difficult for anyone to track your online activities.

Employing Tor in your routine Internet usage can significantly enhance online anonymity. If you often access websites that track user behavior, using Tor can keep you hidden from these invasive practices. Tor can also be useful for reporters and activists working in hostile environments, safeguarding them from surveillance, tracking, and cyber threats.

# 10.4. Heightening Security with Tails OS

Consider this: the Dark Web also incorporates unique operating systems, such as Tails OS, an operating system renowned for its comprehensive security features. Tails directs all its Internet connections through Tor, makes sure no unencrypted data is written to the hard disk, and leaves no traces on the device after use.

For those seeking enhanced security, using a privacy-focused operating system like Tails (for sensitive data processing) or Qubes (for segregating different activities) can be beneficial. Even in our regular Internet usage, these strategies allow for compartmentalization of activities, preventing a single security breach from gaining access to all your data.

# 10.5. Anticipating Threats through Onion Routing

The practice of "onion routing" adds layers of encryption, much like the layers of an onion, obscuring the original data. Fundamentally, it is used by privacy-centric browsers like Tor to defy tracking.

To improve your digital footprint's security, use privacy-focused Internet browsers that support onion routing like Tor Browser. They come with features such as tracking protection, defense against fingerprinting, and automatic deletion of browsing history.

These insights gleaned from the Dark Web might seem intimidating at first glance. However, they prove pivotal in effecting substantial improvements in our online security and privacy. Implementing these practices doesn't endow you with criminal intentions or necessitate your immersion into the Dark Web's murkier corners. Instead, it hands you the tools to protect yourself in an era where digital threats are ever-evolving, helping secure your digital life.

# Chapter 11. The Future of the Dark Web: Predictions and Implications

We stand on the peak of an enigma, gazing down with trepidation and fascination as we dare to speculate about the future of the Dark Web. It's an uncertain trail fraught with speculative assumptions and educated guesses, but one that's imperative to undertake. Will the Dark Web continue to grow, or might it contract under the pressure of global cybersecurity measures? Would it evolve to shield its activities still further, or might it somehow serve a positive, transformational role in society's future? As with all predictions, these remain a blend of sober analysis and hopeful conjecture.

## 11.1. The Expansion of Dark Web

We anticipate an increase in the usage of the Dark Web in the coming years. Advancements in technology will likely equip a wider number of users with the tools and knowledge to access this hidden facet of the internet. Coupled with the growing public dissatisfaction with mainstream internet's monetizing personal data, the expected rise in Dark Web usage is hardly surprising.

However, expansion comes at the price of increased scrutiny. Hence, the battle between individuals maintaining their privacy, and enforcement agencies disrupting illicit activities, is expected to ramp up.

# 11.2. Futuristic Technologies and Their Influence

Futuristic technologies such as quantum computing and AI hold key implications for the Dark Web. These technologies can both aid illicit activities while providing powerful tools to combat them. On the one hand, the unparalleled processing power of quantum computing threatens to render current encryption methods obsolete. This could lead to a more secure and impregnable Dark Web, making the task of uncovering illicit activities increasingly challenging.

On the contrary, these same technologies could empower law enforcement agencies. Quantum computing could crack cryptographic codes presently perceived as unbreakable, while AI could help uncover patterns and connections beyond human capacities to detect. As such, the balance of power could shift dramatically in favor of law enforcement agencies, potentially transforming the landscape of the Dark Web entirely.

# 11.3. The Evolution of Legislation and Privacy Policies

As the Dark Web grows in prominence, so too will calls for governmental regulation and intervention. We expect to see increased international cooperative agreements among law enforcement agencies seeking to curb the illegal activities common on the Dark Web. Such agreements will likely encompass policy changes and legal amendments, focusing on strengthening global online security without impeding upon the right to privacy.

However, this complex task is not without its challenges. Striking a balance between privacy rights and cybersecurity could fuel political and societal debates. It may force nation states to redefine their legislation on internet usage, digital rights and privacy policies, and press multinational tech companies to do the same.

## 11.4. The Emergence of a More Positive Dark Web

Even as we discuss the shadowy aspects of the Dark Web, it's worthwhile to remember that this hidden part of the internet also carries potential for positive change. It's conceivable that as more people start valuing data privacy and taking measures to protect their digital identities, a 'lighter' and more positive aspect of Dark Web might emerge.

For instance, the Dark Web already hosts platforms for whistle blowers, political activists, and journalists working under repressive regimes that limit freedom of speech. These platforms provide necessary anonymity to individuals who, under normal circumstances, would not have their voices heard. Future technological innovations might provide new ways of utilizing the Dark Web for positive social impact, creating a dichotomy between its current perception and its potential future role.

## 11.5. Conclusion

Contemplating the future of the Dark Web is a journey filled with uncertainty. However, by analyzing emerging trends and technologies, we can form an educated forecast. The Dark Web may grow larger, become more secure, face increased legislative scrutiny, and perhaps, serve a positive societal role. The specifics, as always, remain veiled in the contours of the future. Technology and society continue their intricate dance, and we, the spectators, remain watchful, hopeful, and ever curious about the future's untold stories.

www.ingramcontent.com/pod-product-compliance
Lightning Source LLC
Chambersburg PA
CBHW060901260726
48661CB00008B/3389